Artful Animals
DOT-TO-DOT

 RAND McNALLY

Artful Animals Dot-to-Dot

Cover Designer: Erika Nygaard
Illustrators: Robert Delaney III, Lee and Mark Fullerton
Cover Illustration: Mark Fullerton
Writer: Christina Sanders
Puzzle Tester: Jacqueline Henkel
Design Production: Erika Nygaard
Product Management Director: Jenny Thornton
Production: Carey Seren

Printed in Canada
April 2017
PO# 54281
ISBN 0-528-01774-8

If you have any questions, concerns or even a compliment, please visit us at randmcnally.com/contact or e-mail us at: consumeraffairs@randmcnally.com or write to:
Rand McNally
Consumer Affairs
P.O. Box 7600
Chicago, Illinois 60680-9915

randmcnally.com

Introduction

Designed to provide a well-deserved break from today's high-tech world, *Artful Animals Dot-to-Dot* offers fun and challenging dot-to-dot puzzles for enjoyment by all ages. Rand McNally—trusted provider of maps, directions and travel tips for over 160 years—brings this fun-filled voyage around the world to you. Each of the 33 stimulating puzzles averages over 850 dots and includes fun facts, allowing you to discover some of the globe's most remarkable residents of the animal kingdom one dot at a time.

Relax while engaging your mind on a journey across the globe.

Get ready to explore!

Roaming the arctic tundra and forests of Scandinavia, Northern Russia, Greenland, Alaska and Canada, these magnificent creatures live in herds of ten to a few hundred. In the spring, super-herds of several hundred thousand animals may even form.

These animals have two coat layers that can be a variety of colors; a soft undercoat and a top layer of hollow hairs, which hold in body heat for insulation in the cold and allow them to float in water if needed in warmer times. Their coats are not the only feature that helps them adapt to the arctic habitat. They have hairy hooves, with two toes and spongy footpads for walking in mud and marshes. In the winter the hooves harden to better grip frozen ground, ice, and snow. In addition, this species has a specialized nose, completely covered in hair that helps warm incoming cold air before entering its lungs. Their keen sense of smell can detect food hidden under snow as well as predators.

The feature for which they are best known are used as a weapon against predators: their antlers. The massive racks of males can measure up to 50 inches long, with a main beam and tines that branch out. Both males and females have antlers, which fall off and grow back larger each year.

These highly intelligent animals live in social groups, known as troops. Typically troops consist of small family groups, but may expand to up to 30 members led by a dominant male. The tight-knit nomadic troops don't tend to stay in the same place long, but instead construct new nests each day.

Ranging in size from 4 to 6 feet tall and weighing up to 450 pounds, these herbivores may also supplement their vegetarian diet with ants and termites. With arms longer than their legs, they use the back of their fingers as extra feet while traveling to forage for food.

Found in rain forests, wet lowland forests, swamps, and fields of Central and West Africa, these animals make their homes in a wide range of elevations, from mountains reaching altitudes of over 14,000 feet to lowlands at sea level. The habitats are separated by the Congo River.

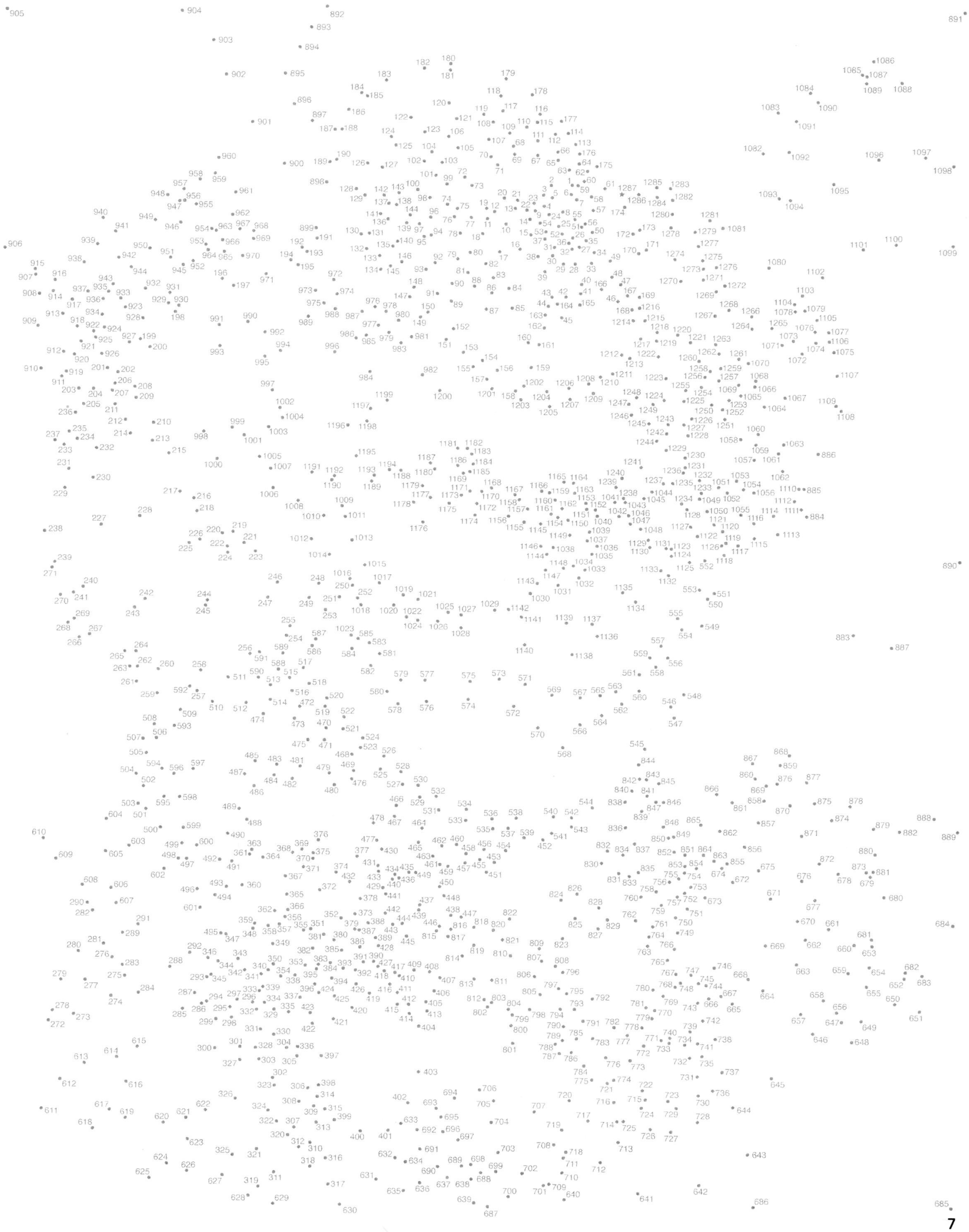

While these strapping beasts reign today in areas south of the Sahara Desert in Africa and in a small region of India, they were much more wide spread in historic times. Their habitats are now almost exclusively centralized in the savannas, dense bush, woodlands and grasslands of Sub-Saharan Africa.

Living in large social groups of three to thirty animals called prides, these animals are tightly connected and rarely welcome strangers. Made up of females and their young with a few unrelated males, once the group is formed the female members stay together for life. Male offspring will leave the pride at maturity.

These beautiful creatures communicate using their famous roars along with scent markings to let other animals know pride's territory boundaries. The pride hunts in groups with the females taking on the main duties. The agile huntresses chase prey towards the center of the group, and they work together to close in on and capture the prey.

The males have manes of hair not only to make them look more impressive to females, but to also serve as neck protection during fights with other males.

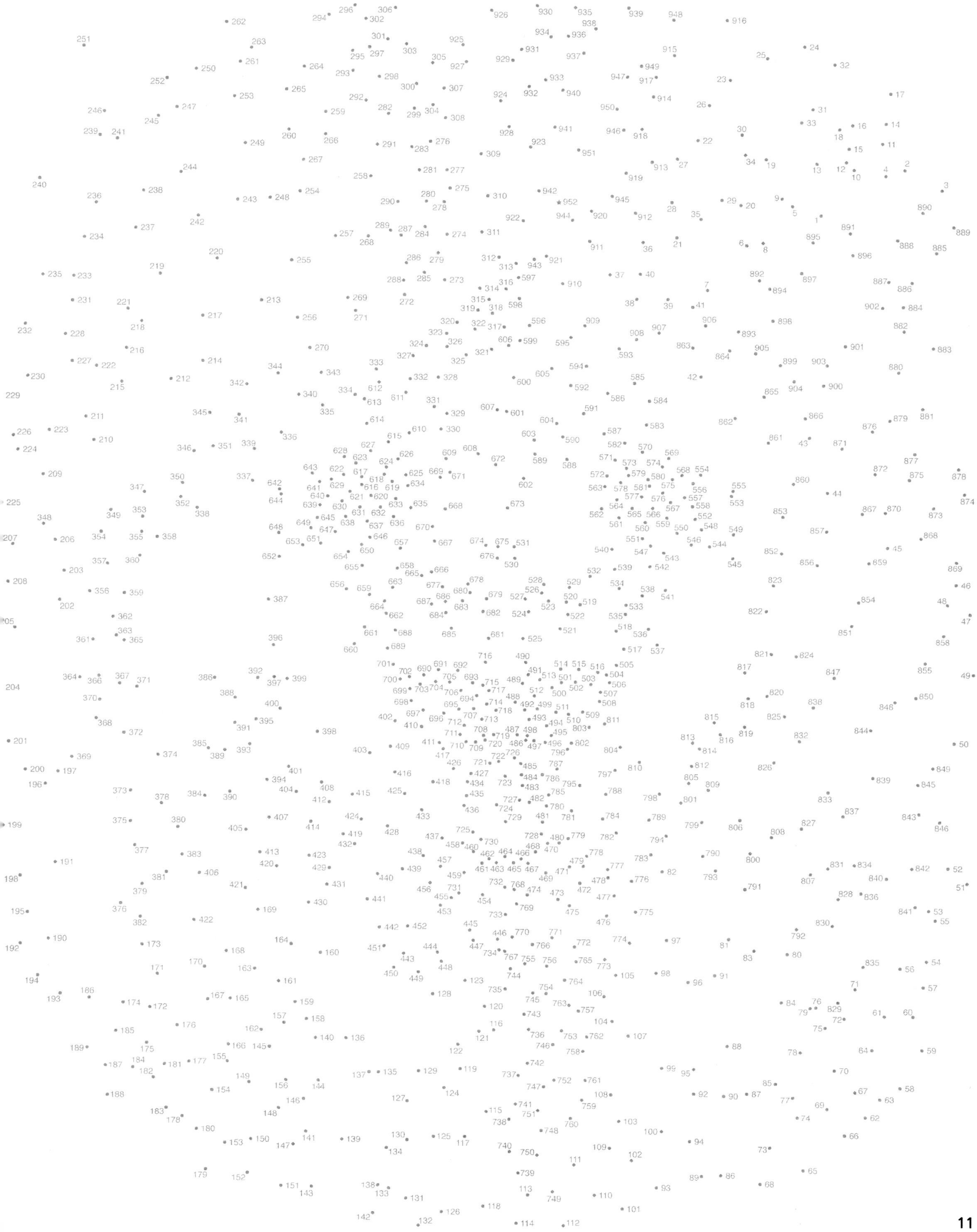

This animal, sacred to the Hindu religion (attributable to the symbolic eyes of gods on its tail), can be found in India, Pakistan, Sri Lanka, Southeast Asia, and Central Africa. Nesting in locations with access to low lying trees and plants, they eat grains, leaves, berries, seeds, flower parts and even small mammals or reptiles.

They are distinguished most by the stunning plumes of the males that fan out in a variety of colors including black, blue, green, gray, red, and orange. The bright feathers not only serve to attract mates, but make them look larger to intimidate predators. Their trains can reach 6 feet long and can be over 40% of their overall body weight.

While the males strut to show off, the females of this species exude a much subtler appearance of drab colors intended to blend into their habitat to better protect their eggs.

Hidden high up in the rain forest canopies of Southern Mexico, Central and South America, and the Caribbean region, these tropical animals make their homes in treetop bands. These non-migratory feathered friends nest in hollowed-out tree cavities, where most live in groups.

They are famous for their large bill made of keratin (the same material as human fingernails), which can be up to four times the size of its head or nearly as long as a third of its total body length. The bill has serrated edges. It is lightweight and mostly hollow except for fibers that support the top. The color of these beaks varies within different species and may be brightly colored greens, reds, whites or yellows, while their main bodies are often mostly black.

They are also a noisy member of the animal kingdom, using vocal calls, barks, croaks and even making tapping and clattering sounds using their bills to communicate and make their presence known.

Mistakenly referred to as bears by early settlers based on their big round ears and general appearance, these marsupials carry their young in a pouch.

Hanging out in the tree-tops of southeastern and eastern Australia (states of Queensland, new South Wales, South Australia and Victoria), these animals surround themselves with eucalyptus trees, which act not only as their primary shelter, but also their main food source. These iconic creatures have hands with sharp claws to dig into bark and two opposing thumbs to assist with gripping branches as they climb and sleep in treetops. They are the only other mammals besides primates to have fingerprints.

Since, these animals need lots of sleep—as much as 18–20 hours per day—to digest their food, these solitary creatures are most active at night and rely on smell to detect predators.

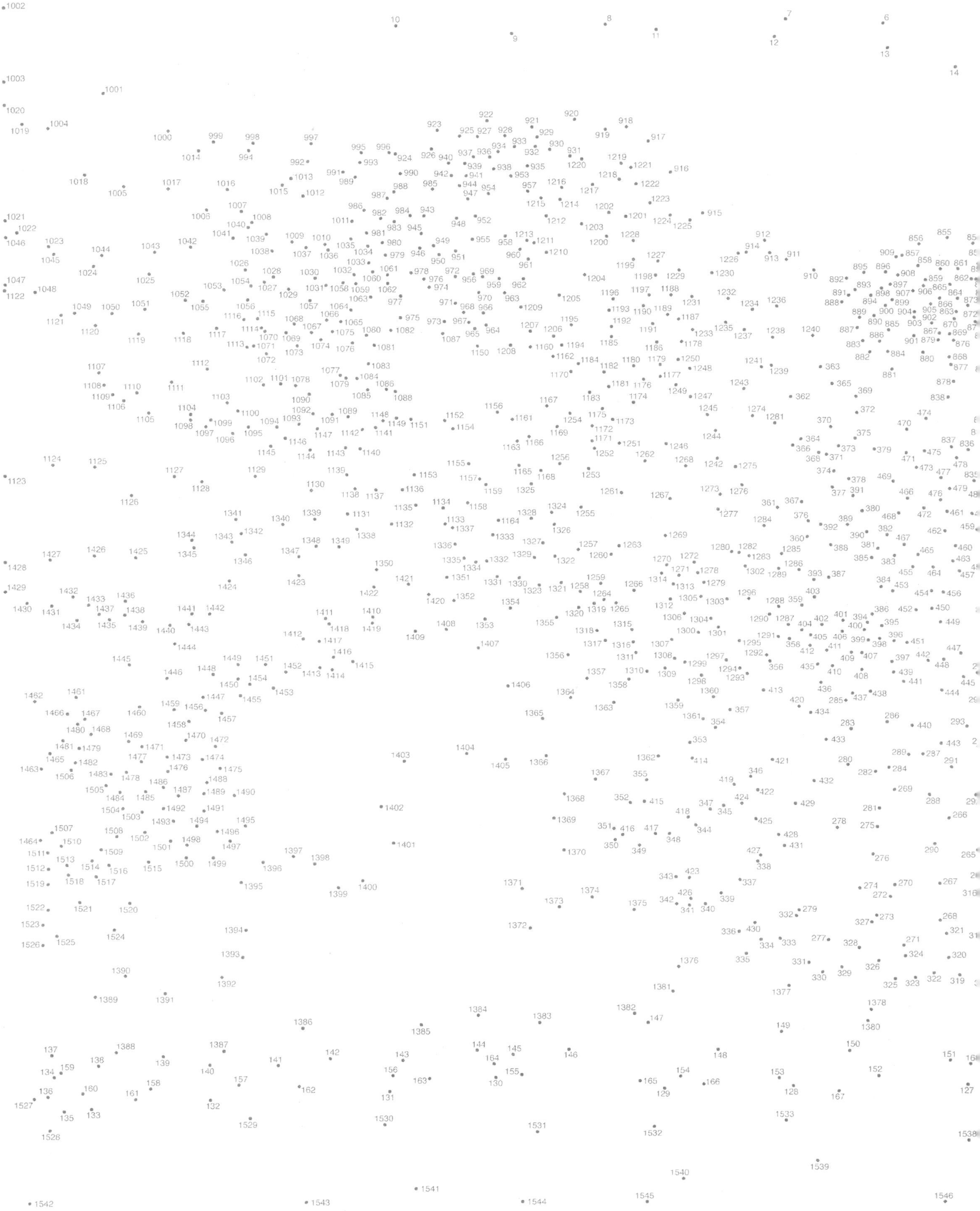

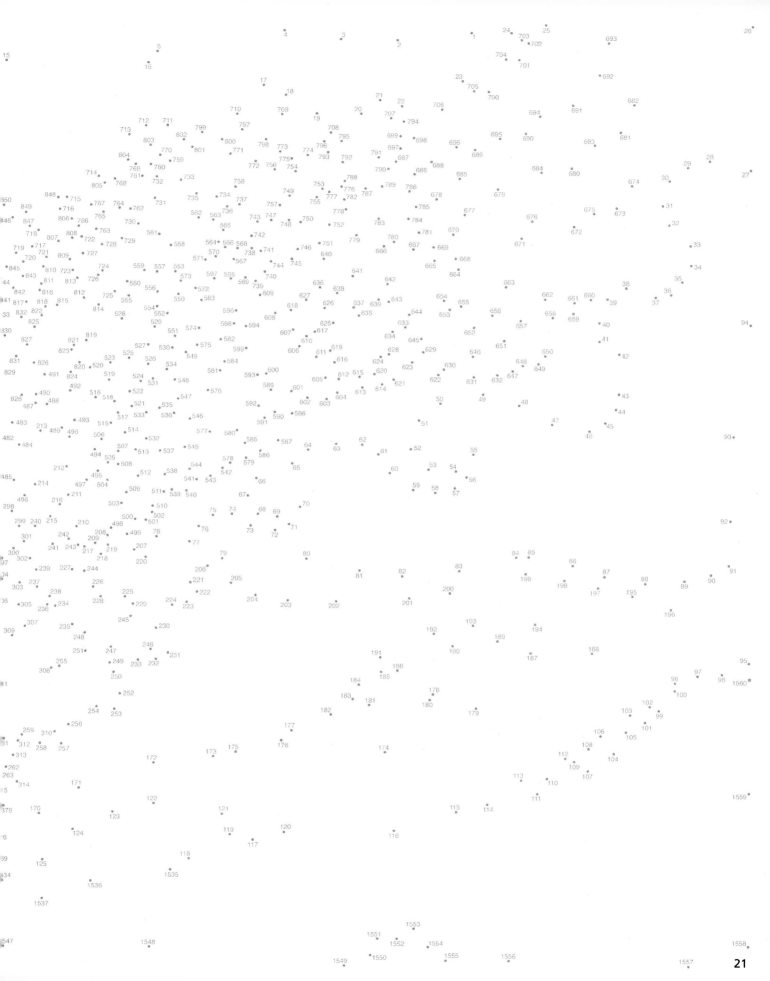

The most populous of any bird, this animal has over 150 different breeds of various colors, patterns, and sizes. Domesticated animals found on every continent except for Antarctica, these feathered friends prefer mild and warm climates.

Don't let their wings fool you, these birds are flightless. Even though they may attempt lift-off by running and flapping their wings, they cannot stay airborne. However, the fluttering efforts might be enough to move short distances such as over a fence.

A male will guard the general area where the females nest, crowing to lay claim on his territory. The guard stance often lends them to perch several feet off the ground for a better view.

The males are recognized for brightly colored plumage, a flowing tail, pointed feathers on their neck, and a large comb atop their heads. Sharp spurs on the back of their legs, which can cause puncture wounds, come in handy for defending their territory from predators. Females typically are not as colorful and lack head combs.

Towering above other mammals—reaching heights of 16 to 18 feet tall—these herbivores can be found dining on the leaves of the highest branches in Africa's tree-dotted plains. As the tallest land animals, their necks alone can be as long as 6 feet and contain seven neck vertebrae, which can each be over 10 inches long. Their long blue-black tongues provide even further extension to ensure that can get a hold of the over 75 pounds of food they consume per day. Not ones to rest on their laurels, these giants require very little sleep, averaging less than two hours per day, allowing plenty of time for roaming for acacia trees.

Natives mostly of Sub-Saharan Africa, different subspecies—indicated by their coat colors and patterns—are found within various countries in Africa ranging from Chad to South Africa.

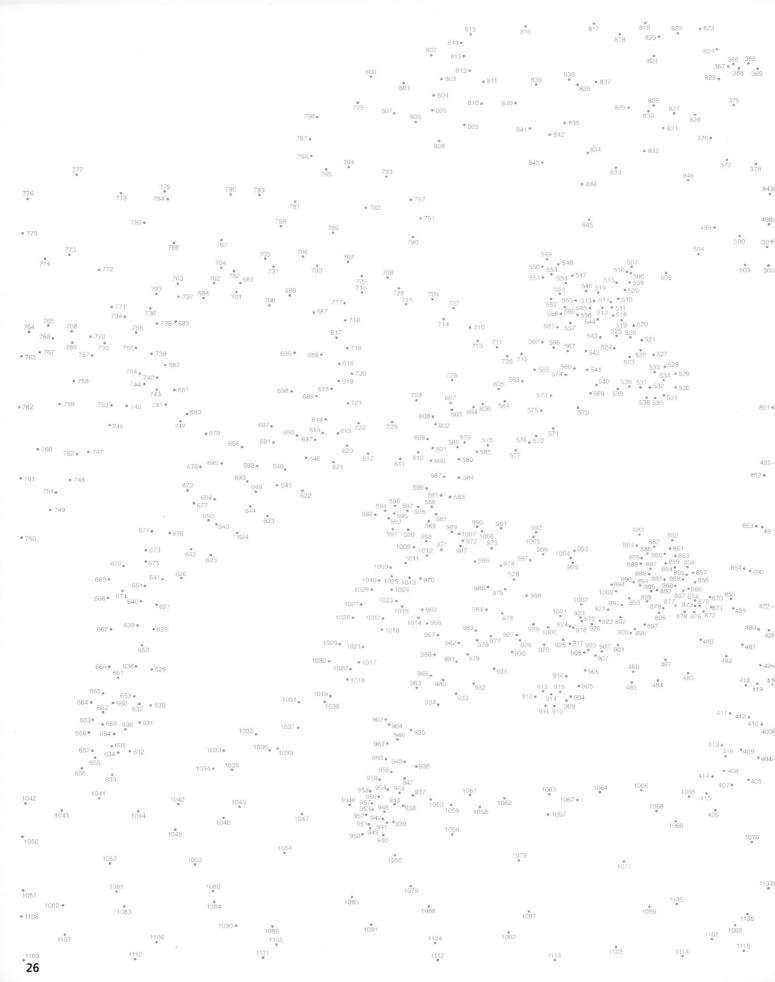

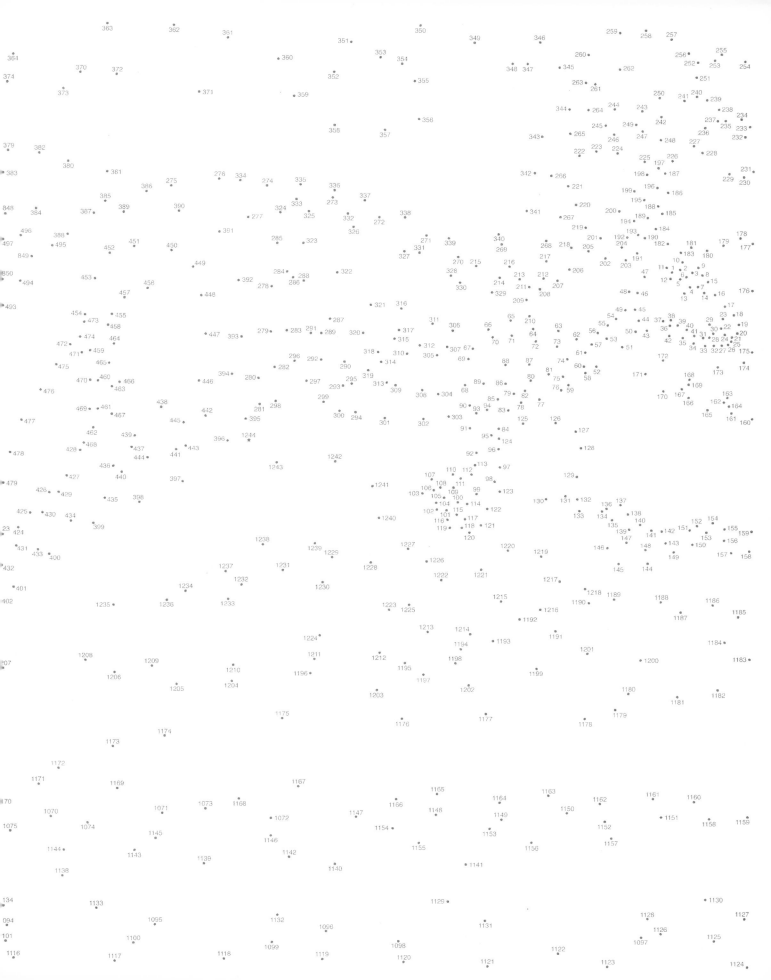

Hiding in the rainforests of southern Mexico, Central America and northern South America, these nocturnal carnivores are named for their ability to climb. These animals tend to gravitate to areas with large amounts of rainfall to protect their highly sensitive skin, which needs to stay moist to avoid drying out.

To safely blend into the rainforest canopy they have a natural camouflage of bright green skin that sometimes includes blue, white and yellow markings, and which may change color based on mood or surroundings. Their red or orange feet have circular suction cup-like discs encompassing their fingers, allowing them to easily grip and climb trees. Beyond their colorful bodies, these animals stand out with bulging red eyes that are protected by a third eyelid membrane. Their outer eyelids match their skin to help them blend into trees while asleep. Once alert, stunning red eyes startle predators by stimulating a ghosting image, buying time for an escape.

Air-breathing reptiles found in all major oceans and smaller seas with the exception of the Arctic Circle, these animals prefer tropical coastal waters and beaches, although some can live in colder waters below 40 degrees Fahrenheit. They can travel hundreds to thousands of miles between feeding and nesting areas; some migrating as far as 1,400 miles.

While they cannot retract their arms or heads into their shells like other members of their animal family, their hard body shell and powerful flippers make them streamlined for swimming. In their 60-80 year life-span these animals spend most of their lives in water, except when laying eggs.

Adult females lay anywhere from 70–200 eggs on the beach, usually near the same nest where they were born, burying the eggs in the sand and returning to sea. The hatchlings emerge from the sand and walk into the ocean to begin their journey at sea.

Of its 7 known species, nearly all are classified as endangered. They range greatly in size with the smallest species averaging 80–100 pounds and the largest tipping the scales at over 1,000 pounds.

Native to warmer climates such as Mexico, Central and South America, the Galapagos Islands, some Caribbean islands (Turks and Caicos), and Fiji, these animals may live in the trees of a tropical rainforest, hidden in deserts, rocky areas, or even in lowland forests.

With over 35 recognized species, they vary in size, behavior and color—from bright vivid hues to dull muted tones. While most are herbivores, some subspecies are omnivores. In all species their tails make up about half of its length. They also have extra skin on their backs called a dewlap to help regulate their body temperature. These unique creatures have a tiny third eye that can sense brightness.

The females lay eggs, cover them and leave the eggs alone to hatch. While the eggs usually hatch together, the young burrow out of their nests and enter the world on their own.

All six subspecies of this imposing beast are now considered endangered. These beautiful creatures dwell in South Asia, Southeast Asia, China, and Russia. From the snowy areas of Siberia to the jungles of Indonesia, the various subspecies may be found in tropical rainforests, evergreen forests, temperate forests, mangrove swamps, grasslands, and savannahs. These animals like to live in areas close to water with an abundance of prey, preferring ranges with dense vegetation to provide cover while hunting.

Best known for their distinct reddish-orange and white coats with black stripes, this coloring acts as camouflage in tall grasses as they await prey. These fantastic beings rely on sight and sound over smell to track mainly large hoofed animals. The solitary hunters then use their three-inch long canine teeth and large jaws to grab onto and secure their next meal. They typically eat as much as possible after a successful hunt, and cover leftovers with grass and dirt to provide smaller snacks over a few days.

Bobbing along the shallow weedy areas and eel grass beds of shallow coastal waters of 52° N to 45° S latitudes, the 54 species vary in size and color according to their watery homes. They are found in various places, from the Pacific waters of North and South America, the Atlantic waters of Nova Scotia to Uruguay, the Mediterranean Sea, and even the Thames River in England.

Surprisingly weak swimmers, these creatures lack caudal fins and use their curly prehensile tails to grip coral or seaweeds so they don't drift off in the currents. Famous for their long downward pointing snouts, this feature acts as a vacuum as they scour for food probing coral reefs, sea grass beds, estuaries and mangroves scouring for food.

Unique to this species; it is the males that give birth. When mating the female transfers her eggs to the male, who fertilize the eggs and carries them in a pouch until they fully develop.

Recognized by their gray or brownish fur, black masks around their eyes, and tails marked with 5-8 black rings, these animals have hind legs longer than their front ones, lending to their crouched stance when on the move.

Their dexterous front paws have 5 finger-like toes that lack webbing between digits. These sensitive paws, while absent of opposable thumbs, still allow them to easily grasp and manipulate objects. Bandit-like in appearance and mischievousness, these nocturnal omnivores will eat almost anything, from crayfish to plants to unattended eggs in nests, as well as the contents of urban garbage cans.

Adaptable to their surroundings, these animals are native throughout most of North America, appearing in northern Canada, the United States, Mexico, even southward into northern parts South America. They have even recently been spotted in parts of Europe and Japan.

While they prefer heavily wooded areas where they can nest in tree holes or fallen logs, they have boldly ventured to nesting in any location they can get into including the attics or crawl spaces of human homes. Once they find a cozy nesting spot, they may go dormant in winter.

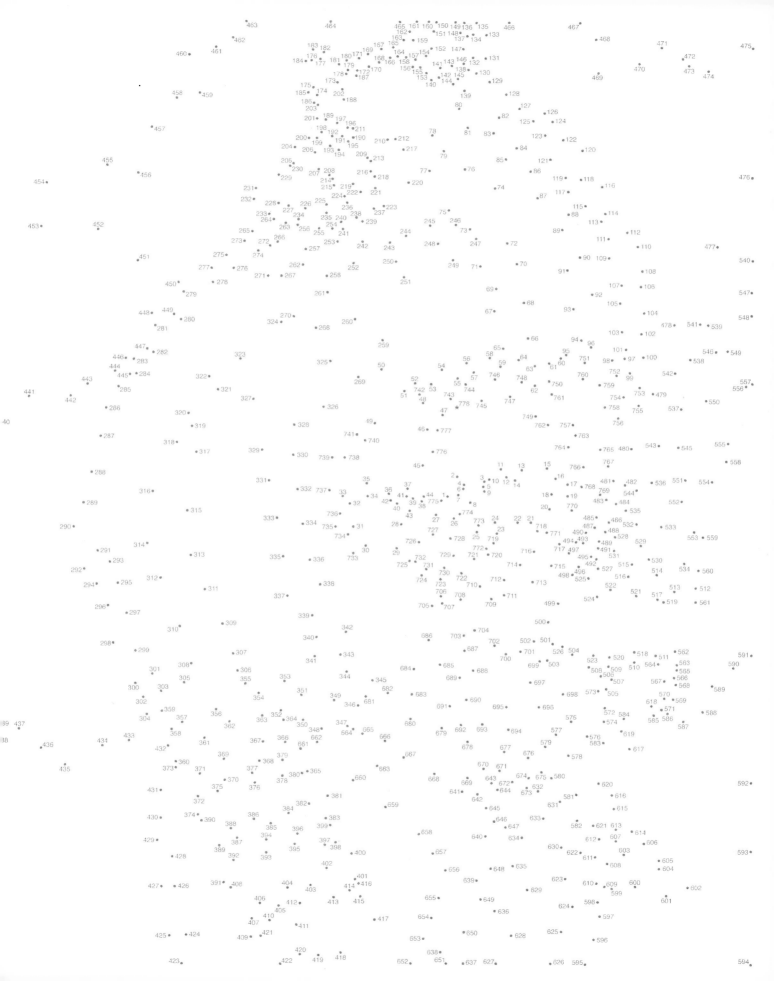

In the vast frozen tundra of the Arctic, these animals blend into the snowy confines of their environment. Attracted to open areas on the shorelines of lakes and oceans, agricultural fields, and prairies, these majestic creatures are occasionally found in forests. They may migrate to find food rather than to escape the cold.

Their bulky bodies and wings spanning 60 inches are covered in dense feathers, even on their legs and talons, to help retain body heat for survival in the colder climate. White coloring helps them blend into their surroundings. However, most females and younger animals are not totally white, having some darker feathers forming spots over their bodies. Males get whiter with age, but only some turn completely white.

These hunters fly low to the ground across the tundra to search for food. Their keen eyesight and incredible hearing help them locate prey under snow and vegetation. While they may prey on rodents, birds and fish, their favorite treat are lemmings.

Fluttering among flowers and plants, more than 18,000 species of this insect are known to exist. They are found in every country in the world, except on the continent of Antarctica and the severest deserts!

Cold blooded creatures, with an ideal body temperature of 86°F, these beautiful winged beings cannot fly if the air temperature dips below 55°F. Since their ideal air temperature for flying is 82–100°F, tropical climates like Hawaii and Mexico host an abundance of the species. Some may even migrate over two thousand miles just to keep in warmer climates at all times.

Warm humid conditions are key to ensuring a steady food source. Unable to chew solids, these animals have an all liquid diet of plant nectars. Drumming leaves with their feet makes plants release juice, which they then taste with a tube-like mouth.

Their most striking feature may appear to be colorful to the naked eye, but their wings are actually transparent. Formed by layers of chitin—the protein that make up insect exoskeletons—the wings are covered by thousands of tiny scales that reflect light of different colors.

Renowned for their unique appearance in the animal kingdom, these animals often have olive green or dark gray coats with yellow and black bands, white bellies, and large canine teeth that can be up to 2 inches long. However, it is their hairless face and elongated snout with blue ridges on top, red noses and lips and brightly colored hind quarters that distinguishes them most.

Found mostly in the rain forests of equatorial Africa— Cameroon, Equatorial Guinea, Gabon, Nigeria, and Republic of Congo—their territory is bordered by the Sanaga River to the north, and by the Ogooue and Ivindo Rivers to the east.

Using their long arms to move around on the ground, days are spent searching for food and new nesting areas. They have large pouches in their cheeks that can be utilized to transport food to new locations for later consumption. Since these animals rarely sleep in the same tree two nights in a row, this extra cargo space comes in handy when it is time to pack up and move.

They live in troops headed by a dominant male, but the smaller units can form into larger groups called hordes. The largest known horde ever recorded had over 1,300 members!

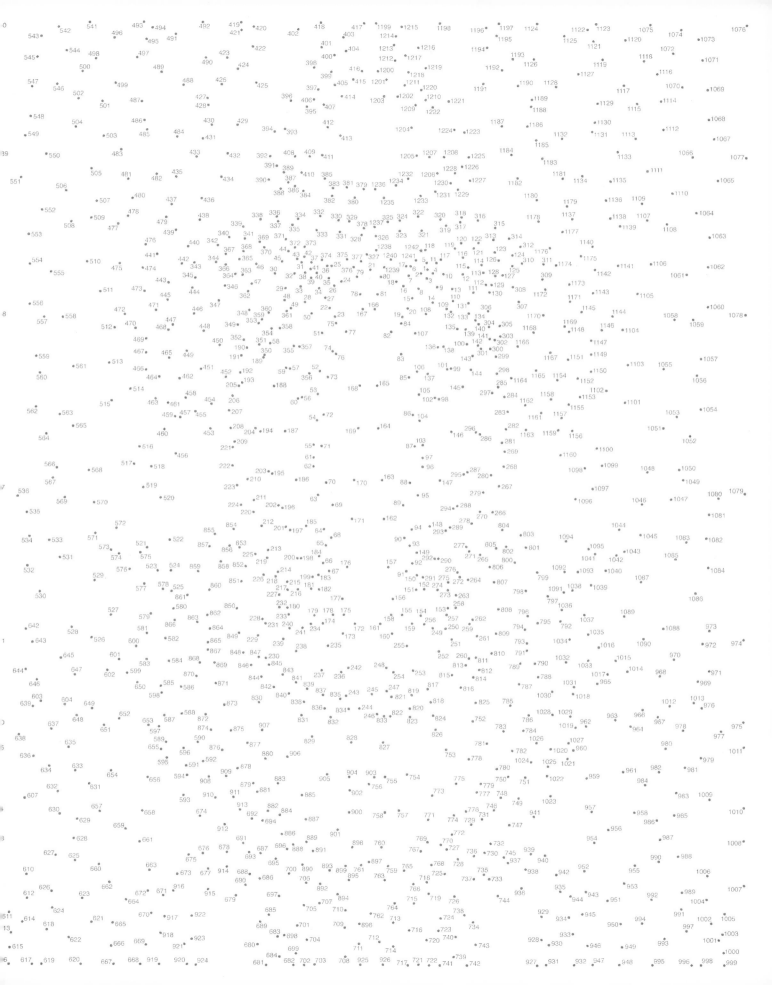

Thought to have been domesticated by the Incas thousands of years ago, these herbivores can be found grazing the Andes, Peru, Ecuador, and the northern part of Chile in South America. They often make their homes in high mountain regions reaching up to 16,000 feet above sea level.

They are primarily raised for their beautiful soft wool coat fibers. These fibers naturally come in over 22 colors and hundreds of shades, combinations, and blends. While their fleece is silky and lightweight, it is also strong, water resistant, and high in insulation, making the byproducts of it highly in demand. Males produce about 8 pounds of marketable fleece per year on average.

Using a variety of noises to communicate—from sharp and high-pitched to low humming sounds—these long-necked creatures live in social herds led by an alpha male. They may spit and kick when feeling vulnerable. Adult males also have incisors and lower canine teeth that can be over 1.2 inches long for further protection from threats.

With over 189 recognized domesticated breeds, man's best friend is found all over the world. This specific breed originated in the southern provinces of China with artistic evidence of their ancestry dating back to the Han Dynasty. These intelligent creatures are thought to originally have been bred as palace guards.

While named for their sandpaper-like rough coats, these animals are recognized most for wrinkled skin around their head, neck, and shoulders that loosens and spreads as they mature. They have small sunken eyes, tiny triangular ears, a broad muzzle, a thick high-set slightly curled tail, and typically weigh about 40–60 pounds. Adding to their distinct appearance, these loyal companions display a blue-black tongue, making them one of only two breeds with this feature.

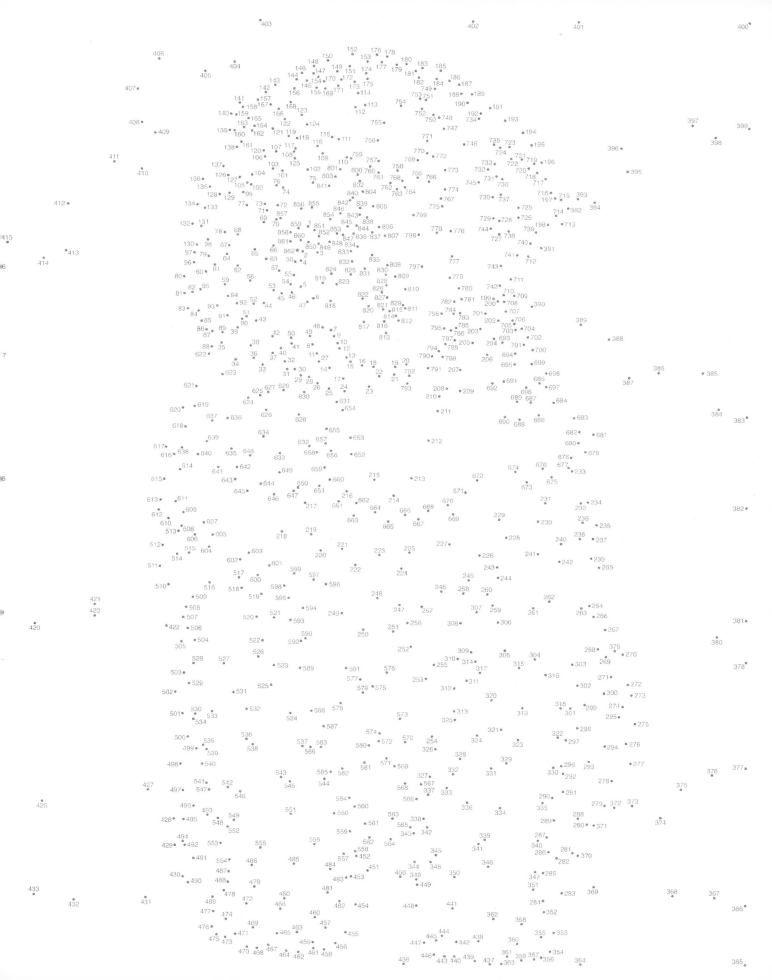

Inhabiting the largest geographic range amongst mammals outside of humans, these animals are found throughout the entire Northern Hemisphere including Europe, temperate Asia, northern Africa, and North America. They have even been introduced in Australia.

Calling wooded areas, prairies and farmland home, the females may make one or more dens after mating. They are mostly nocturnal, but they may hunt during the day. These omnivores prefer rodents, but will eat birds, amphibians and fruit. Their specialized hearing allows them to pick up low frequency sounds, so they can even hear their favorite prey digging.

These sly creatures are identified by their reddish brown coat of long guard hairs with a soft fine underfur, long bushy white-tipped tails, black ears and legs.

With a life span of only 3-4 weeks and over 20,000 different species, these slinky creatures can be found all around the world in a multitude of habitats including sandy beaches, meadows, mountain forests, and even some Arctic areas.

Even though they vary greatly in size, color and appearance, they all use their appearance to disguise and protect themselves for the next stage of life. Each has 6 true legs and up to 5 pairs of false prolegs to help them climb. They also have 12 eyes, with 6 eyelets on each side of their heads that can only discern light and dark.

The only job of this creature is to consume enough fuel to gain energy for metamorphosis. Some species can consume up to 27,000 times their body weight, molting their skins multiple times to accommodate their size during the growth period, while going through 5 stages of development before moving onto the next phase of their lives.

Found only in Madagascar and the nearby Comoro Islands off of the Southeast coast of Africa, these playful animals have over 100 species. Madagascar's varying ecosystems range from high mountains in the center of the island to rain forests and semi-deserts on its edges, giving rise to the diversity of the sub-species. They range greatly in size depending on their species, from 1 ounce to 20 pounds. With bright round eyes and soft fur, most species have tails that are longer than their bodies.

These intelligent members of the primate order are highly social, living primarily in family groups or troops. A dominant female will often lead groups indicating when it is time to move, eat, rest and groom. They use scent markings and alarm calls to communicate and notify others of predators in the area.

These animals can be found hopping through the thick scrublands and dense forests of the coastal regions of Australia, Papua New Guinea, and Tasmania. Solitary nocturnal herbivores, they hide in the underbrush and tunnel through bushes to search for leaves, grass, seedlings, and shoots. They can reach speeds up to 34 mph.

With seven different species found in various regions, these small marsupials range in size from about 16 to 20 inches and weigh anywhere from 7 to 26 pounds. Their fur can be brown, red, black, grey or a combination of these colors.

Their young are born thirty days after mating and then spend six months developing inside the mother's pouch.

SOLUTIONS

PAGE 5: Reindeer

PAGE 7: Gorilla

PAGES 8–9: Parrots

SOLUTIONS

PAGE 11: Lion

PAGE 13: Peacock

PAGES 14–15: Zebras

SOLUTIONS

PAGE 17: Toucan

PAGE 19: Koalas

PAGES 20–21: Eagle

SOLUTIONS

PAGE 23: Rooster

PAGE 25: Giraffes

PAGES 26–27: Kangaroos

SOLUTIONS

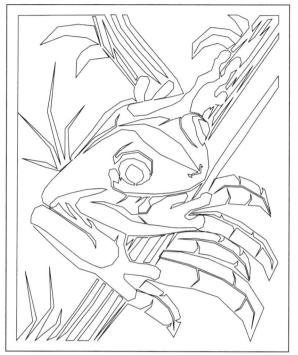

PAGE 29: Frog

PAGE 31: Sea turtle

PAGES 32–33: Penguins

SOLUTIONS

PAGE 35: Iguanas

PAGE 37: Tiger

PAGES 38–39: Mandarin

SOLUTIONS

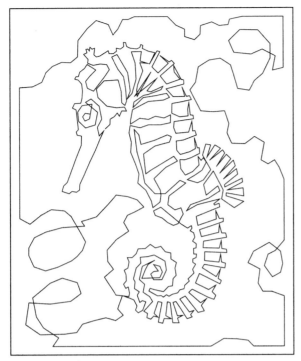

PAGE 41: Seahorse

PAGE 43: Raccoons

PAGE 45: Snowy owl

PAGE 47: Butterfly

SOLUTIONS

PAGE 49: Mandrill

PAGE 51: Alpaca

PAGE 53: Shar pei

PAGE 55: Red fox

SOLUTIONS

PAGES 56–57: Elephants

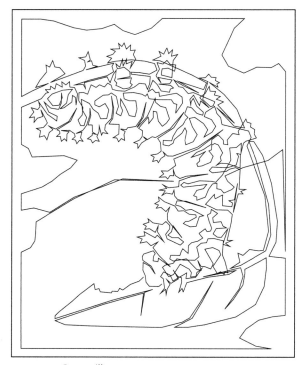

PAGE 59: Caterpillar

PAGE 61: Lemur

SOLUTIONS

PAGES 62–63: Pandas

PAGES 64–65: Mountain sheep

SOLUTIONS

PAGES 66–67: Fish

PAGE 69: Pandemelon